Stefanie Hoffmann

CW00591901

Classical Motivation Theories - Similarities and Differenc

Stefanie Hoffmann

Classical Motivation Theories - Similarities and Differences between them

GRIN Verlag

Bibliografische Information der Deutschen Nationalbibliothek: Die Deutsche Bibliothek
verzeichnet diese Publikation in der Deutschen Nationalbibliografie; detaillierte bibliografische Daten sind im Internet über http://dnb.d-nb.de/ abrufbar.

1. Auflage 2006
Copyright © 2006 GRIN Verlag
http://www.grin.com/
Druck und Bindung: Books on Demand GmbH, Norderstedt Germany
ISBN 978-3-638-84102-3

University of Wales Institute, Cardiff

**Classical motivation theories –
Similarities and differences between them**

by
Stefanie Hoffmann

Submitted for:
B.A. (Hons) International Business Management

Contents

List of Figures

1. Introduction

"We always do what we MOST WANT to do, whether or not we like what we are doing at each instant of our lives. Wanting and liking many times are not the same thing. Many people have done what they say they didn't want to do at a particular moment. And that may be true until one looks deeper into the motivation behind the doing. What they are really saying is the price they will have to pay or the consequences they will have to endure, for not doing that something may be too high or onerous for them not to do it. Such as going to work. Many people say they don't want to go to work and yet they do. Which means they don't want to risk losing their jobs and the negative hurting emotions associated with not having a job. It has been estimated about 90% to 95% of all people work at jobs which are unfulfilling and which they dislike and would leave in a minute if they only knew what they really wanted to do."

Sidney Madwed

(http://www.quotationspage.com/search.php3?homesearch=motivation accessed on 15.02.2006)

The quotation defines that nowadays motivation should be an indispensable part of every company. It is a complex and difficult topic and therefore management also has to take historical theories into account. Furthermore, it has to be figured out what employees designate as attractive for defining an effective motivation programme within the organisation.

This dissertation will critically evaluate what motivation is and illustrate the different kinds of motivation theories of Abraham Maslow, Frederick Herzberg and Clayton P. Alderfer by explaining the key concepts for managing and motivating people. Due to the fact that motivation, especially employee motivation, is such a broad topic the dissertation will put a specific focus on the similarities and differences between the classical motivation theories.

2. Methodology

This dissertation was first of all intended to evaluate the similarities and differences between classical motivation theories.

It was the researcher's intention to concentrate particularly on the work of Abraham Maslow, Frederick Herzberg and Clayton P. Alderfer as the motivation theories which have been established by them are the most famous ones.

Secondary Data Collection

Research was initiated by reading books, journals as well as newspaper articles in order to obtain a theoretical framework for the research topic.

Furthermore, relevant books and electronic resources, for example Internet articles and journals were used to gather information and to broaden the range of secondary research.

Primary Data Collection

A primary research of this topic would not have been possible due to the required time to elaborate and carry out a meaningful survey. Furthermore, primary data research such as questionnaires or interviews would not have been sufficiently representative for the intended purpose.

3. What is motivation?

Motivation is a psychological process and it can be explained as the willingness of individuals to do something for satisfying a need. A need is a psychological or physiological deficiency, which makes the attainment of specific outcomes attractive. Unsatisfied needs lead to drives which generate a search for particular goals. If these goals are attained the need will be satisfied. (Robbins and Coulter, 2002) In everyday life, people ask themselves the question why they do some things or why not. In response, individuals try to find a motive which justifies the behaviour. Motives form the basis of needs. Therefore, it can be said that people seek for solutions in order to solve deficiency which means that motives are activated. These incentives may derive from us or they can come from other persons. Motivation is divided in two different types. The first one is called intrinsic motivation which means that people engage in an activity for its own sake, for example pursuit of responsible activities or personal development potentialities. Extrinsic motivation is used by a third party, for example supervisors or managers to motivate employees with either tangible rewards (payments, promotions, punishments) or intangible rewards (praise, public commendation). (Steers, Porter and Bigley, 1996)

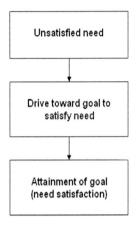

Figure 1: The basic motivation process (Hodgetts and Luthans, 1997, p. 332)

There are a lot more definitions of motivation but all have in common that motivation is a psychological process influencing internal motives which direct behaviour of a person and force him to activity with the intention to reach some objectives. Most psychologists believe that motivation is ultimately derived from a tension that results when one or more of people's important needs are unsatisfied. Therefore, a person who is hungry is motivated to find food or a person who needs security is motivated to find it. Another important point called behaviourism has to be taken into consideration concerning motivation. Behaviourism has its roots in 1953 when B. F. Skinner explored that people learn through their experiences and that these affect who and what they become. (Weightman,1999) Furthermore, he stated that people will most likely engage in desired behaviours if they are positively reinforced for doing so and rewards are most effective if they immediately follow the desired response. Skinner was also mainly responsible for the development of the philosophy of neo behaviourism and for the further progression of applied behaviour analysis, a branch of psychology which aims to develop a unified framework for animal and human behaviour based on principles of learning. The psychologist did not support the use of punishment because in his opinion it is an ineffective way of controlling behaviour and that a behaviour that is not rewarded or is punished is less likely to be repeated. (Skinner, 1974) It is said that the exploration of the emotional and motivational life of the mind is one of the greatest achievements in history of human thought. Furthermore, psychological motivation defines that individuals tend to seek pleasure and avoid pain which means that people want to maximise positive results and minimise the negative ones. Therefore, motivation energises, directs and sustains behaviour.

The expectancy theory of motivation which describes how individuals make decisions regarding behavioural alternatives has also become a commonly used theory. It defines that people have different set of goals and that they can be motivated if they believe that there is a positive connection between efforts and performance, that the performance will result in a good remuneration, that this remuneration will satisfy a special need and that the wish to satisfy this need is strong enough to make the effort worthwhile. (Vroom, 1964) While other theories of motivation provide a theoretical framework for thinking and understanding what motivates people in the workplace and everyday life, the expectancy theory deals with practical solutions concerning diagnosing and solving individuals' motivation problems.

Concerning the expectancy theory, motivation is a combination of valence, instrumentality and expectancy. Like mentioned above, motivating people by showing them worthwhile outcomes and then supporting them to reach these goals or desires helps people or employees to act in a way that provides pleasure and avoids pain. (Green, 1992)

In addition, humans are motivated by many things, for example psychological needs, emotions, hurts, impulses, fears, rewards such as money, friendship or status, wishes, intentions, values, self-satisfaction, interests, pleasure, dislikes, goals, ambitions and so on. An employee who is motivated works better than one without motivation. It is also known that people are ready to work harder if they see that their work is rewarded. Therefore, managers must know how to motivate their employees in order to complete tasks and achieve the goals of the company by applying motivation theories. There are many different approaches of motivation. The work of three well-known psychologists called Abraham Maslow, Frederick Herzberg and Clayton P. Altderfer is closely associated with human needs and motivation and helps to create better living and working conditions.

4. Why is motivation so important in management?

"The only way to get people to like working hard is to motivate them. Today, people must understand why they're working hard. Every individual in an organization is motivated by something different." Rick Pitino

(http://www.yourquotations.net/author/Rick%20Pitino.html accessed on 25.02.2006) Motivation is closely linked to the performance of human resources in modern organisations but it must be remembered that although the motivation process may be the same across cultures, the content of what motivates people is often different. In modern management there is a multitude of concepts which aim at the attitudes of employees and managers. These concepts not only provide motivation in the sense of increasing performance but also the loyalty and commitment of employees to the organisation. Most of the modern concepts concerning human resource management are founded on motivational basics. In today's economic situation the survival and the success of an organisation depend on efficiency and innovative ability. Therefore, the employee is the most crucial source because if he is able to identify himself with the aims and objectives of the company, productivity and innovation will be increased.

Motivation theories concerning management also have a historical context. One theory that some companies used was the scientific approach which was put forward by Frederick Taylor, an American engineer. It was mainly applied in the late 1800's and early 1900's, during the time of industrialisation and increasing mass production.
Taylor developed his theory while he was working his way up from a labourer to a manager. The theory comprises that man is a rational economic animal

concerned with maximising the economic gain. The model also assumes that human beings are simply motivated by monetary incentives and that they have no interest in the contents and tasks of their activity. For that reason, Taylor concluded that to increase production, managers must take control of the work processes which means that the workers had an influence on the execution of their work but had no possibility to make decisions. (Taylor, 1947) The basic principle that is underlying his approach is that if people study what happens when they change different variables in a situation this will tell them how to organise the workforce in the best way. Scientific Management exists of different techniques that are also used today called:

- "Scientific method of doing work"
- "Planning tasks"
- "Standardization"
- "Specialisation and division or work"
- "Time and motion studies"

(http://en.wikipedia.org/wiki/Motivation_theories accessed on 25.02.2006)

Nevertheless, nowadays companies try to move away from scientific management but it is still applicable in menial industries such as assembly lines and fast-food restaurants. The principles are often used when managers analyse the basic work tasks that must be performed when they hire the best suitable workers for a job or when managers use time-and-motion studies to eliminate wasted motions. (Robbins and Coulter, 2002)

In some respect, it is obvious that Taylor's theory is out of date due to the fact that people do not just work for money. They also work for socialisation and factors like earning respect from fellow employees or managers.

The Human Relations Model which was created by Elton Mayo is also very significant concerning motivation in management. He believed that workers could be motivated by acknowleding their social needs. Moreover, making the employees feel important would improve the conditions at work. The model named "Hawthorne effect" was created in order to push foward the start of Human Relations Movement in management and organisational thinking. With the help of his experiments, Mayo wanted to show the limits of precision of Taylor by discovering the effect of different intensities of lighting on the production line and on the productivity of its staff. (Robbins and Coulter, 2002)

Finally, Mayo and his engineers found out that if the level of light became more intensive also the level of output increased and that employees got more motivated as soon as they noticed that they got more attention than before. As a result, employees were given more freedom to make decisions on the job and greater attention was paid to informal work groups. Moreover, the results of the Hawthorne model led the researchers to question what other changes in working conditions could improve the output. It is outlined that being part of a group or having a certain status within it often means more to an employee than pay or better working conditions. As a conclusion, Mayo noticed that production was increased without motivating employees by rewards and remuneration, which had been taken into consideration by

Taylor. Furthermore, he saw that employees began to enjoy their tasks and that social relationships outside work became more and more important.

(http://www.managers-net.com/hawthorne.html accessed on 02.03.2006)

Nowadays, motivation is one of the most important and frequently debated issues in organisational behaviour. It is stated, that whether you are a mananger or someone being managed, motivation is a prime concern and of considerable social and economic significance. There are of course various reasons why companies are interested in motivationg their employees. It is said that poorly motivated staff tends to underperform whereas in all activities well motivated individuals and teams are an important ingredient of success. Motivated individuals tend to work with greater effort and condfidence and enjoy high productivity. Additionally, motivated employees are more satisfied with their work and therefore their environment.

5. Motivation theories

"A person's motivation, job satisfaction and performance is determined by the strength of their needs and expectations and the extend to which they are fulfilled."

(http://ferl.becta.org.uk/content_files/ferl/resources/organisations/rsc_scotland /joan_walker/motivational_theories.ppt#1 accessed on 04.03.2006)

The basic motivation concepts can be divided into process and content theories. Process theories are more focused on individual behaviour in specific settings. It explains how employee behaviour is initiated, redirected and halted whereas content theories explain motivation in terms of what arouses, energises or initiates employee behaviour. (Hodgetts and Luthans, 1997) However, it is important to remember that none of the following theories have been conclusively shown to be valid. Nonetheless, they are helpful in providing a contextual framework for dealing with individuals, in general and at the workplace.

Content theories are more useful to create a detailed picture of work motivation because they regard motivation in more general terms.

For that reason, the focus is set on the content theories of Maslow, Herzberg and Alderfer.

5.1 Abraham Maslow - Hierarchy of human needs

Abraham Maslow was one of the most important representatives of the humanistic psychology which had a high influence among organisational psychologists and the study of organisational behaviour.

One of the main interesting things Maslow noticed was that some needs take precedence over others. It is demonstrated that if people are hungry or thirsty, they tend to try and take care of the thirst first. After all, people can live without food for several weeks, whereas water is dispensable just for a few days. Maslow took this idea and created the well-known hierarchy of human needs.

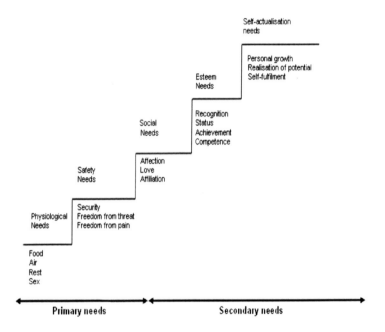

Figure 2: Maslow's hierarchy of human needs (Weightman, 1999, p. 39)

Beyond the details of air, water, food and sex he laid out five broader layers. These layers are physiological needs, safety and security needs, the needs for loving and belonging, esteem needs and self-actualisation. The physiological needs include requirements people have for oxygen, water, salt, sugar or other minerals.

There are also needs to be active, to sleep or to avoid pain. Maslow believed that when physiological needs are largely taken care of, the safety and security needs layer comes into existence. People become increasingly interested in finding safe circumstances, stability and protection. They might develop a need for structure, for order or some limits. Looking at it negatively, people might become concerned, not with needs like hunger or thirst, but with their fears and anxieties.

When physiological and safety needs are mostly taken care of, the love and belonging needs layer starts. People begin to feel the need for friends, family, affectionate relationship in general and even a sense of community. The negative side to this is that they may become extremely susceptible to loneliness and social anxieties. Concerning self-esteem, Maslow noticed two versions of esteem needs, a lower one and a higher one. The lower one is the respect of others, the need of status, fame, recognition, reputation, appreciation or even dominance. In contrast to the lower need, the higher form involves the need for self-respect, including feelings such as confidence, competence, independence or freedom.

(Maslow, 1987)

The last level is difficult to describe. Therefore, Maslow used a variety of terms to define this level called self-actualisation. These are needs that do not involve balance. Once engaged they do not disappear, they continue to be felt. In fact, these needs are likely to become stronger as people feed or stimulate them. They involve the continuous desire to fulfil potentials as well as the drive to become what a person is capable of becoming. If people truly want to be self-actualised they need to have all their lower needs at least mostly fulfilled. It is obvious that the specific form of these needs varies from person to person. Nowadays, it is still a challenging problem for research. As satisfied people are the exception of our society, people do not have much information about self-actualisation. Furthermore, there is an individual variation in the degree to which self-actualisation can be a motivator. Firstly, it is a learnt, culturally determined need and secondly, like mentioned above, the other needs must be satisfied first. (Maslow, 1987) In conclusion, Maslow described the human action in form of stepped needs which come from a holistic and positive idea of man. In Maslow's opinion the needs of human beings are arranged like a ladder with the most basic needs at the bottom and self-actualising needs at the top. The psychologist illustrated that unfulfilled needs at the lower level would inhibit the person from coming to the next level of the ladder.

First of all, Maslow's motivation theory is a theory of personality development. While assigning his theory in organisations there were many people who critically appraised the adoption of it. Initially, Maslow did not conceive his hierarchy for the workplace but nevertheless it is possible to adjust it. Thus, his hierarchy of human needs was also the first major theory of motivation to be applied to individuals at work.

Physiological needs are needs, which people must satisfy to keep alive. Applied to the work environment, these needs are often satisfied through basic salary paid by the company. Safety needs include the desire for security. In the work place, they involve ensuring personal safety and income by providing security through retirement plans, medical insurance or similar benefits. Social needs include the desire to interact with other people as well as receive and give friendship. On the workplace this can be obtained in informal or formal groups. Esteem needs are, for example the needs for status or power. At work this could be fulfilled through a company car or an important position. Self-actualisation needs are desired to make the fullest use of one's potential and to develop oneself. In the work environment this class seems to be hard to satisfy. The people who are most likely to satisfy these needs are, for example skilled workers or managers. (Hodgetts and Luthans, 1997) According to Maslow, if each of these needs is substantially satisfied, it is no longer motivating and the next level of the hierarchy becomes dominant. This means, that a higher need will only become active, if the lower needs are satisfied.

Figure 3: Meaning of the hierarchy of human needs at the workplace (Steers and Porter 1991, p. 3)

Experts do not agree in the point if to support or to refuse Maslow's theory. The following paragraph will define the different meanings and opinions of well-known researchers, psychologists and scientists.

Some studies found that Maslow's hierarchy was the same, or at least very similar in other cultures, while others found significant differences in the hierarchy. Haire, Ghiselli and Porter undertook a study to examine the importance of Maslow's four highest level needs. Therefore, they surveyed managers from 14 countries. The only modification of Maslow's hierarchy was that the esteem need was divided in two segments, prestige and self-esteem as well as autonomy. The first examined the importance of esteem and the second the significance of authority and the possibility for independent thought and action. The result of the study was that the importance of all the needs depend on the culture. For some surveyed managers, for example from the USA or the United Kingdom, the upper level needs like self-actualisation and autonomy were the most important ones. (Hodgetts and Luthans, 1997)

Also Geert Hofstede, a well known Dutch researcher, suggests that Maslow's need-satisfaction profile is not a sufficient way of addressing motivation. Due to various cultures, it may be nearly impossible to determine how individuals rank their needs at work in any particular work setting. Furthermore, Hofstede stated that job categories are a more successful way of examining motivation. In his opinion, there is a correlation between different kinds and levels of jobs and Maslow's hierarchy of human needs. (Hofstede, 1991)

Also the historian and political scientist James McGregor Burns analysed Maslow's approach to motivation in regard to the development of leadership.

"Few other motivational theories matched Maslow's in boldness and intellectual creativity. His theory had the virtues of clarity, economy, and flexibility, without sacrifice of comprehensiveness. Unlike the Freudians,

Maslow was above all an optimist. Not only did he describe ultimate human potential in the most generous terms of self-actualization, he held that people were powerfully motivated to achieve that potential." (Burns, 2003, p. 148-149) According to Burns, Maslow's hierarchy of human needs had a remarkable meaning because of the important connection between his drive for self-actualisation and the motivation for leadership. The scientist also believed that flexibility, creativity and openness which characterise self-actualisation were very similar to the criteria of leadership. (Burns, 2003)

Another researcher said that "Maslow's theories are attractive because they provide a practical and understandable picture." (Wooldridge, 1995, p.17) The only concern which exists is the adaptation to the work environment. Due to the difficult current economic situation, many companies and especially their employees had to undergo different entrepreneurial changes which made it hard to realise self-actualisation. Therefore, it would be a great solution to find a way to satisfy higher order needs without meeting the lower order ones which means "to stand Maslow's hierarchy on its head" would stimulate creative thinking and action. (Wooldridge, 1995)

As a result, the model of Maslow cannot be confirmed as the satisfaction of people is not measurable. The hierarchy of human needs has often been criticised for several reasons. Like already mentioned above, there is a demur concerning the content of the hierarchy. With regard to self-actualisation, Maslow views it as the ultimate need. For those who reach this highest level, it involves being what people are most capable of being. "A person becomes what he is most capable of becoming. What a man can be, he must be." (Maslow, 1943, p. 370) Another concern of the hierarchy of human needs is that the needs of individuals should be seen as dynamic rather than static. It is obvious that needs are changing depending on the situation people are involved. In conclusion, Maslow's theory comprises that an essentially satisfied need is not a motivator. In general, this is true but special needs are never permanently satisfied. (Whittington and Evans, 2005)

It is important to understand Maslow's rank order of needs not as a fixed and inflexible structure. In general, the behaviour of people is defined by several needs and motives so that an overlapping concerning these motives and needs can not be excluded. To be concluded, Maslow's theory is controversial but affords an opportunity to have a critical look at what is important or non-relevant for oneself. Nevertheless, he anticipated that his work would eventually lead to a "periodic table" of the kinds of qualities, problems and even solutions, characteristic of higher levels of human potential. Over time, he got increasing attention, not to his own theory, but to humanistic psychology and the human potentials movement.

5.2 Frederick Herzberg - Two factor theory

Frederick Herzberg and his colleagues developed the two factor model of motivation in the workplace in the so called Pittsburgh study. Herzberg was the first to show that satisfaction and dissatisfaction at work depend on different factors. Therefore, his work became one of the most replicated theories in the field of workplace psychology.

He simplified Maslow's hierarchy of human needs into two distinct dimensions, the hygiene factors and motivators which affect people's attitude at work. Thus, his study is also often called the motivation-hygiene theory. (Hodgetts and Luthans, 1997)

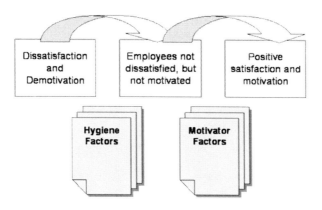

Figure 4: Motivation-hygiene theory

(http://www.tutor2u.net/business/images/herzberg_factors.gif accessed on 20.03.2006)

"Ask your employees to define work. If they say, "It's what I do for money",

you could be in trouble." (Buchanan, 2004, p.19)

People talk about work in many ways. Therefore, Herzberg wanted

employees to think about their attitudes to their place of employment. In

general, there is a great variety of estimating job attitudes. In the first part,

employees had to answer questions if they like or dislike their job which again

depends on several factors, for example age, sex, educational level or the

position in the company. It was and is crucial not to measure just the general

attitude to the job but also the feelings about specific areas of employees'

work. In the second part, scaled inventories of job attitudes had been taken

into consideration. These inventories are based on the assumption that it

would be possible to combine many specific responses concerning the attitude to work and to achieve an over-all score that expresses the employee's moral. In the third approach, the behaviour of workers was observed which derived from their feelings or motives. The last point can also be compared to the Hawthorne study, which was already mentioned in the third part of this dissertation.

(Herzberg, Mausner and Bloch Snyderman, 1993)

Nevertheless, the two basic questions:

- "When did you feel particularly good about your job?"
- "When did you feel exceptionally bad about your job?"

were the basis for the development of Herzberg's motivation-hygiene theory.

(Hodgetts and Luthans, 1997, p. 339)

The first question refers to satisfaction at the workplace, especially achievement, recognition, responsibility, advancement or the work itself. These factors are also called motivators (intrinsic) and are based on an individual's need for personal growth. When they exist, these factors create job satisfaction and they can motivate an individual to obtain high-quality performance and effort.

The second question aimed at factors like salary, technical supervision, company policies and administration, interpersonal relations or working conditions.

These hygiene factors (extrinsic) are based on the need of an organisation to avoid unpleasant working conditions as they can create dissatisfaction of employees which again leads to a bad company performance.

HERZBERG'S TWO-FACTOR THEORY	
Hygiene factors	**Motivators**
Salary	Achievement
Technical supervision	Recognition
Company policies and administration	Responsibility
Interpersonal relations	Advancement
Working conditions	The work itself

Figure 5: Herzberg's two factor theory (Hodgetts and Luthans, 1997, p. 340)

The salary of employees is taken as a special example. The income as a hygiene factor safeguards the livelihood and is therefore an incentive for working. The income level is closely connected with the status of the employee. A salary increase is classified as recognition of the professional success. But money can also compensate for missing interpersonal relationships. However, if the income has reached a certain level to finance rent, clothes, a car or vacation, an increase in salary hardly contributes to raise the employment of labour as it seems to be the most natural thing in the world due to habituation.

The two factor theory comprises, like the other content theories, that the power of motivation is only defined by an unsatisfied need which will be illustrated in the following figure.

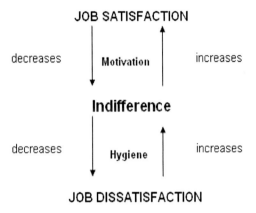

Figure 6: Own illustration: Motivators and hygiene factors depending on job satisfaction and dissatisfaction

It can be said that hygiene factors deal with the conditions which surround the execution of work. They demonstrate the employee that the environment in which he performs his task is unfair and disorganised. If there is a decrease of hygiene factors, job dissatisfaction arises. It has also been taken into consideration that if the working conditions are acceptable, dissatisfaction may still be possible. Motivators which lead to contentedness satisfy the employee's need for self-actualisation in his work. It is highlighted that if the satisfying motivators are missing it does not lead to dissatisfaction but only to non-dissatisfaction. Motivators which are involved in the development of job satisfaction are different to the hygiene factors which lead to job dissatisfaction. Therefore, job satisfaction and job dissatisfaction are not the opposite of each other. The opposite of job satisfaction is non-job satisfaction and the opposite of job dissatisfaction is non-job dissatisfaction.

(Neuberger, 1974)

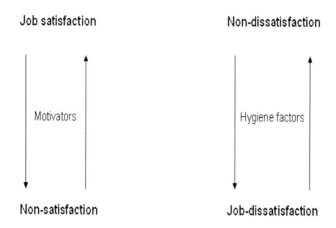

Figure 7: Motivators and Hygiene factors with its dedicated opposites (Neuberger, 1974)

Neuberger compares job satisfaction with seeing and job dissatisfaction with hearing. Thus, it deals with two different senses which do not influence each other. (Neuberger, 1974)

Herzberg also believed that business should motivate employees by improving the content of the job through certain methods. Some of the methods he suggested are job rotation, job enlargement, job enrichment and empowerment.

(http://www.tutor2u.net/business/gcse/people_motivation_theories.htm accessed on 25.03.2006) Job rotation deals with the movement from one job to another in order to increase skills and to avoid boredom. Job enlargement means that the number of tasks which are done by the employees should be increased in order to make the work more interesting and diverse. A good example to describe that statement is the American restaurant chain TGI Fridays. Besides serving meals and drinks, employees must entertain the guests at their table. Thus, there is a greater variety of tasks to perform which improves the daily work routine of the employees. Job rotation and job enlargement do not have their roots in any psychological theory but the attempts to redesign jobs have been developed by Frederick Herzberg. In addition, job enrichment comprises an increase in the decision making process which means that more responsibility is given and that workers have a wider range of more complex, interesting and challenging tasks. Empowerment is the concept of encouraging and authorising employees to take the initiative of improving operations as well as product quality and customer service. Also the delegation of more power to employees in order to make own decisions in different areas of the company defines this term. (Weightman, 1999)

It is evident that if workers are not satisfied with the conditions of their work it may lead to:

- "Low productivity"
- "Poor production or service quality"
- "Strikes / industrial disputes / breakdowns in employee communication and relationships"
- "Complaints about pay and working conditions"

(http://www.tutor2u.net/business/people/motivation_theory_herzberg.asp accessed on 25.03.2006)

In conclusion, management must not only provide hygiene factors to avoid unpleasant working situations and employee dissatisfaction but also must provide intrinsic factors or motivators in order to reach satisfaction of the workers. Herzberg stated that the different methods mentioned above are required for intrinsic motivation and that it must be a continuous management process in order to reduce the number of de-motivated employees.

Apart from the two factor theory, Herzberg is also known for his acronym KITA which has been politely translated as a kick in the pants. The theory comprises punishing, threatening or rewarding employees in order to improve productivity and quality in an organisation. Herzberg was convinced that KITA does not produce motivation but movement. In the article "One more time: How do you motivate employees?" which was originally published in the Harvard Business Review in 1968, Herzberg tries to answer one of the most important questions in management: "How do I get an employee to do what I what him to do?". He explains that the easiest thing in order to realise this question is to ask the worker. If he does not want to do the task the next step would be to give him a kick in the pants. As a result the worker will complete the order as it is his duty, but this action will not lead to motivation, it will only lead to movement.

(http://www.maaw.info/ArticleSummaries/ArtSumHerzberg68&03.htm accessed on 27.03.2006)

There are different terms of KITA. Negative KITA in general means motivation by punishment and is again divided in negative physical KITA and negative psychological KITA. The first term commonly appeared in the past and as the physical attacks that had been used directly stimulated the autonomic nervous system it resulted in a negative feedback and is illegal today. In the second term, cruelty is not visible and the person who is involved has the possibility to be above it. Nevertheless, there is no tangible evidence of an attack and the employee can also be accused of being paranoid. Moving to an undesirable office or threaten termination are examples with which managers try to make use of negative psychological KITA. Positive KITA is in general motivation by reward. Many businesses offer workers incentives like compensation or benefits to meet or exceed targets. (Herzberg, 2003) As a conclusion, none of the approaches led the employees to take the initiative by themselves as, because of external pressure, the workers are prompted to a certain behaviour. From the manager's point of view it would mean: "I am motivated; you move!" (Herzberg, 2003, p.88)

According to Herzberg, managers can create conditions which motivate their employees such as giving them interesting tasks, more responsibility or a positive feedback. Furthermore, managers should deactivate dissatisfying factors by providing reasonable payment or a better working atmosphere. However, Herzberg's theory has also been criticised. It is said that his two factor theory is the most controversial theory of work motivation. There are people who do not agree with the division of the several factors, for example that the salary belongs to the hygiene factors because it is commonly argued that money is a primary motivator. David Guest has said: "Many managers' knowledge of motivation has not advanced beyond Herzberg and his generation. This is unfortunate. Their theories are now over 30 years old. Extensive research has shown that as general theories of motivation the theories of Herzberg and Maslow are wrong. They have been replaced by more relevant approaches." (Armstrong, 1999, p. 50) The most critical points of Herzberg's theory are:

- big parts of the theory are formulated vague and ambiguous so that an empirical refutation of the basic statements is impossible
- the differentiation between hygiene factors and motivators is just possible with the help of the interview method
- the individual differences in the need structure have been considered in an inadequate way

(Wunderer and Grunwald, 1980)

Also Herzberg's research, procedures and methodology have been criticised. It is said that his research is flawed and fails to support the contention that money or pay is not a motivator. Furthermore, he did not make any attempt to measure the correlation between satisfaction and performance. (Armstrong, 1999)

Another criticism is whether Herzberg has developed a total theory of motivation. There are many people who argue that his results and findings actually support a theory of job satisfaction which means that if a company offers its employees motivators, such as more responsibility, they will be satisfied, if the company does not do it, dissatisfaction arises. If the hygiene factors are inadequate, people are dissatisfied too. (Hodgetts and Luthans, 1997)

In the international arena there have been a number of studies in order to investigate the different attitudes concerning Herzberg's two factor theory. The result was that in many countries the motivators were of more importance concerning job satisfaction than the hygiene factors. Also for people who hold management positions, job content factors, such as responsibility, achievement and the work itself are more important than job context factors, such as earnings, benefits or promotions. It is demonstrated that managers from other countries differ concerning the importance of job outcomes and the degree of satisfaction experienced on the job with respect to these outcomes. These findings are useful in order to find out what motivates managers in other countries, and multinational companies have the opportunity to develop human resource management approaches, adapted to the individual country. (Hodgetts and Luthans, 1997)

As a conclusion, Frederick Herzberg's two factor theory has been both, influential and controversial. His ideas really shaped modern thinking about reward and recognition in many companies but the most important point which has to be taken into consideration is that all people have different habits and attitudes and that the results of Herzberg's theory cannot be applied to all human beings.

5.3 Clayton P. Alderfer - ERG-theory

The ERG-theory is a model that was created in 1969 by Clayton P. Alderfer. It appeared in a Psychological Review article named "An Empirical Test of a New Theory of Human Need". In reaction to Abraham Maslow's need hierarchy, Alderfer differentiated between three categories of human needs that influence employee's behaviour: **E**xistence needs, **R**elatedness needs and **G**rowth needs.

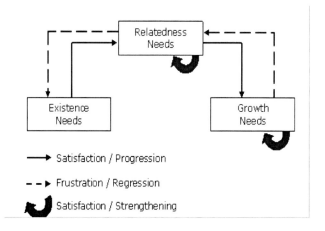

Figure 8: Alderfer's ERG-theory

(http://www.valuebasedmanagement.net/methods_alderfer_erg_theory.html accessed on 10.04.2006)

Existence needs comprise physiological and safety needs, for example security, food, air or sex which can be compared to Maslow's first two levels of his hierarchy. Achievement, recognition or the relationship with family or workers belong to Alderfer's second classification, the relatedness needs which are similar to Maslow's third and fourth part of the pyramid. The last level called growth needs includes strive for self-actualisation and internal esteem. These desires of personal growth and realisation of potential explains Maslow in the fourth and fifth part of the hierarchy of human needs. (http://www.valuebasedmanagement.net/methods_alderfer_erg_theory.html accessed on 11.04.2006)

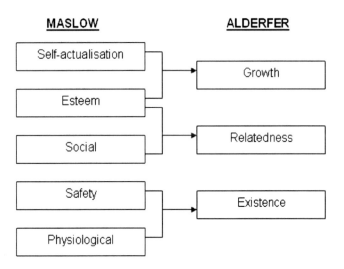

Figure 9: Own illustration: Comparison of Maslow and Alderfer

The aim of Alderfer was to define the statements of Maslow in conjunction with organisations. Therefore, he developed his ERG-theory because he believed that companies and managers need to make use of all of his three needs. Alderfer also stated that where for example growth is not possible at work the other two needs must be used in a more powerful way.

(Weightman, 1999)

Furthermore, Alderfer said that growth needs would inhibit people to make creative and productive efforts for themselves.

"Satisfaction of growth needs depends on a person finding the opportunities to be what he [or she] is most fully and to become what he [or she] can." (Armstrong, 1999, p. 363) As a result, people will seek and find ways for themselves and companies have to put a special focus on providing growth and development. If the organisation does not give such opportunities, people will go away and grow maybe in another company.

The empirical work of Alderfer is based on questionnaires which have been completed by managers, students and industrial workers. These questionnaires provided indications of satisfaction and desires for the existence-, relatedness- and growth needs. (Alderfer, 1972)

Like mentioned above, in his analysis Alderfer makes use of only three need levels. The reason for that is that he saw the risk of an overlap between safety-, social- and esteem needs. Alderfer expands the theory of Maslow in different ways. Furthermore, the following principles and models have to be taken into account:

- Frustration-model: **P1**

  An unsatisfied need becomes dominant.

- Frustration-regression-model: **P2**

  If some needs cannot be satisfied, the individual's focus is redirected to other, more achievable lower level needs.

- Satisfaction-progression-model: **P3**

  Because of the satisfaction of a need, the next one on the hierarchical higher level is activated.

- Frustration-progression-model: **P4**

  An unfulfilled or unsatisfied need is the trigger that a need on a higher level becomes urgent.

Starting from these principles mentioned above, Alderfer drew the following conclusions:

- The less existence needs are satisfied, the stronger they become. **G1**

- The less relatedness needs are satisfied, the stronger existence needs become. **G2**

- The more existence needs are satisfied, the stronger relatedness needs become. **G3**

- The less relatedness needs are satisfied, the stronger they become. **G4**

- The less growth needs are satisfied, the stronger relatedness needs become. **G5**

- The more relatedness needs are satisfied, the stronger growth needs become. **G6**

- The more growth needs are satisfied, the stronger they become. **G7**

(Rosenstiel, 1992)

The fundamental statement is that the stronger a need is perceived, the less it is satisfied.

The following figure will demonstrate the interaction between the needs among each other.

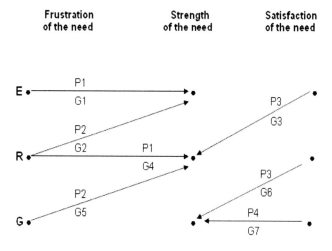

Figure 10: Classification of needs (Rosenstiel, 1992, p. 371)

According to these models or hypotheses it is possible to recognise why employees who have, for example poor opportunities for advancement are more interested in factors like salary or other operational benefits.

A good example for the frustration-model would be a chief executive manager of a big company. He resigns from the job as he is bored of his tasks and as he wanted to do more challenging and creative things. Hence, his needs were not satisfied in the position as a CEO.

The satisfaction-progression-model can be explained by a man who sold his company in order to have more privacy and time for the family. But after a certain period of time the man became active and enthusiastic again and consequently he founded a new enterprise.

Also Alderfer's ERG-theory has been criticised. It has been discovered that needs can be structured in a hierarchical order. The difficulties lie in the general confusion about needs or motives because all people have different attitudes concerning the structure and the intensity of their needs. Furthermore, it has to be said that the individual need structure of a person is changeable. It is not the case that always the same needs are dominant and that the dominant needs always have the same strength.

6. Similarities and differences between the motivation theories

The theories of Maslow, Herzberg and Alderfer are considered classics in organisational behaviour. First of all it has to be said that the most important similarity is that all theories mentioned above are content theories. This term is defined as: "The theories of motivation associated with the forces within us (desires, drives and needs) are categorised as ´need theories´ or ´content theories´ ... (and) concentrate on the inputs of motivation." (Petzall, Selvarajah and Willis, 1991, p. 52) Content theories go as for back as the turn of the century when Scientific Management School proposed sophisticated wage incentive models. Followed by the human relations movement, the content models of Maslow, Herzberg and Alderfer emerged.

Figure 11: Theories of motivation, (Luthans, 1989, p. 239, slightly changed)

Furthermore, content theories explain why human needs change with time and they put a special focus on what motivates human beings.

Frederick Herzberg's two factor theory is closely linked to the hierarchy of human needs of Abraham Maslow. He continued the work of Maslow but entirely related it to the workplace. Herzberg divided Maslow's pyramid into a lower level and a higher level set of needs and suggested that the best way to provide motivation for an employee is to offer him higher order needs such as esteem and self-actualisation. Furthermore, Herzberg, Maslow and also Alderfer stated that needs have to be satisfied for the employee in order to be motivated. The following figure illustrates the linkage and similarity between both theories.

Maslow's need hierarchy	Herzberg's two-factor theory
Self-actualization	Motivators
	Achievement
	Recognition
	Responsibility
Esteem	Advancement
	The work itself
Social	Hygiene factors
	Salary
	Technical Supervision
Safety	Company policies and administration
	Interpersonal relations
Physiologic	Working conditions

Figure 12: Relationship between Maslow and Herzberg (Hodgetts and Luthans, 1997, p. 340)

It can be seen that as Herzberg's motivators are psychological they can be compared to the last two levels of Maslow's pyramid. Herzberg stated that his hygiene factors which aim at the environment, can be assigned to the lower level needs of Maslow's hierarchy and that they can only cause dissatisfaction if they are not addressed. (Hodgetts and Luthans, 1997) For Herzberg, adding more hygiene factors to the job is a bad way to motivate employees because lower order needs are quickly satisfied. It means that salary or rewards will not inspire employees if their basic needs are not met. Alderfer extended the work of Herzberg and particularly that of Maslow.

In order to compare the ERG-theory with Maslow's hierarchy of human needs, Alderfer conducted an interview with 110 employees at several job levels in a bank. He found that none of the satisfaction scales, formed by summing the individual items, showed significant interrelations in the direction predicted by Maslow. Therefore, the results tended rather to support the ERG-theory more than the one of Maslow, although Alderfer did acknowledge that he was researching in a single organisation and that it was impossible to know what special conditions in that organisation may have led to the particular outcomes. (Alderfer, 1972)

Alderfer's theory exists of three needs, existence-, relatedness- and growth needs. The existence needs are similar to Maslow's physiological and safety needs. Relatedness needs can be compared to Maslow's esteem and social needs which means that, for example affection, affiliation or recognition play an important role. Like the model of Maslow, the theory of Alderfer is structured hierarchically. It means that existence needs have priority over relatedness needs which again have priority over growth needs. The hierarchy of human needs works on the same principle.

The main difference between Maslow's and Alderfer's theories is that Maslow believed that unfulfilled needs at a lower level would inhibit a person from coming to the next level of his hierarchy whereas Alderfer argued that different needs may exist simultaneously and that although a need is satisfied it may continue to dominate. Furthermore, the ERG-theory comprises that people can change the order of needs based on their individual desire and attitude.

(http://www.netmba.com/mgmt/ob/motivation/erg/ accessed on 20.04.2006)

In contrast to Maslow's satisfaction-progression-model, the ERG-theory includes a frustration-regression-model whereas those who are unable to satisfy a higher need become frustrated and regress to the next lower level.

In comparison to the two factor theory of Herzberg, it can be seen that the existence- and relatedness needs of the ERG-theory are similar to the hygiene factors of Herzberg and that the growth needs can be equate with the motivators. Alderfer believed that needs are moving backwards and forwards and not just upwards in the hierarchy. In addition, the model of Alderfer allows more flexibility, and the Herzberg model is useful as an explanation for job satisfaction and as a point of departure for practical application.

The following summarises the basic details of Maslow, Herzberg and Alderfer in an abridged version:

- **Maslow:** Argues that lower order needs must be satisfied before one progresses to higher order needs
- **Herzberg:** Hygiene factors must be met if a person is not satisfied. They will not lead to satisfaction, however. Motivators lead to satisfaction.
- **Alderfer:** More than one need can be important at the same time. If a higher order need is not being met, the desire to satisfy a lower level need increases.

In conclusion, each theory describes the physiological, psychological and self-actualisation aspects in almost identical terms. Herzberg's hygiene factors mirror Maslow's physiological, safety and social needs and Alderfer's existence and relatedness needs. Maslow's esteem and self-actualisation needs are similar to Herzberg's motivator traits and Alderfer's growth requirement. It should be clear that the similarities vastly outweigh the differences. It has to be outlined that all motivation theories mentioned in this dissertation were and are a remarkable piece of social science that is still influential and applied.

7. Conclusion

This dissertation has represented and examined the major motivation theories of Abraham Maslow, Frederick Herzberg and Clayton P. Alderfer. It can be concluded that these theories offer some good proposals for managers and organisation concerning how to motivate and lead employees. Furthermore, it can be seen that the different models are a powerful instrument to improve management and therefore the performance of the company. However, it is important to notice that the needs of individuals vary to some degree, depending on social background, attitudes, values or beliefs. Also the occupation and the position of the employee have to be taken into consideration concerning motivation in companies and organisations.

"The only lifelong, reliable motivations are those that come from within and one of the strongest of those is the joy and pride that grow from knowing that you've just done something as well as you can do it." Lloyd Dobens and Clare Crawford-Mason

(http://www.quotationspage.com/search.php3?Search=Motivation&startsearc h=Search&Author=&C=mgm&C=motivate&C=classic&C=coles&C=poorc&C=l indsly accessed on 24.04.2006)

This quotation strongly clarifies that it is difficult to find out what motivation theory is the best to be applicable and which factors are likely to be the most effective and powerful ones. In addition to this, it is obvious that all the theories cannot fully explain all aspects of human behaviour. Petzall, Selvarajah and Willis stated that a lot of research has already been carried out but still "we know almost nothing on the subject." (Petzall, Selvarajah and Willis, 1991, p. 143)

Finally, it can be summarised that employee motivation is one of the most significant and challenging tasks of management. The theories which have been represented in this dissertation clarify that it is not enough to satisfy the physiological basic needs. Motivation is affected by a multitude of factors, which can mostly not be generalised. Every human being is different in his personal view, his hopes, desires and preferences. Therefore, the individuality of the employees is important as it is connected with the meaning and the significance of motivation in the organisation. The most important ability a company must have is to be sincere and consistent in its motivation techniques. Recognising and understanding employees' needs should be an indispensable part of every organisation. Also the acknowledgements of good work will contribute to achieve the desired behaviours.

References

Books

Steers, R.M., Porter, L.W. and Bigley, G.A. (1996) Motivation and leadership at work, London: McGraw-Hill

Hodgetts, R. and Luthans, F. (1997) International Management, New York: McGraw-Hill

Weightman, J. (1999) Introducing Organisational Behaviour, Harlow: Longman

Skinner, B.F. (1974) About Behaviourism, London: Jonathan Cape Ltd.

Vroom, V.H. (1964) Work and motivation, New York: McGraw-Hill

Green, T.B. (1992) Performance and Motivation Strategies for Today's Workforce, Oxford: Greenwood Publishing Group

Taylor, F.W. (1947) Scientific Management, New York: Harper & Brothers

Robbins, S.P. and Coulter, M. (2002) Management, Upper Saddle River, New Jersey: Prentice Hall International

Maslow, A. (1987) Motivation and Personality, New York: Harper & Ro

Steers, R.M. and Porter L.W. (1991) Motivation and Work Behaviour, London: McGraw-Hill

Hofstede, G. (1991) Cultures and Organisations – Software of the Mind, London: McGraw-Hill

Burns, J.M. (2003) Transforming Leadership – The Pursuit of Happiness, New York: Atlantic Monthly Press

Herzberg, F., Mausner, B. and Bloch Snydermann, B. (1993) The Motivation to Work, New Brunswick, New Jersey: Transaction Publishers

Neuberger, O. (1974) Theorien der Arbeitszufriedenheit, Stuttgart: Kohlhammer

Armstrong, M. (1999) Employee Reward, London: Institute of Personnel and Development

Wunderer, R. and Grunwald, W. (1980) Fuehrungslehre – Grundlagen der Fuehrung, Berlin: Walter de Gruyter & Co

Alderfer, C. (1972) Existence, Relatedness and Growth, New York: The Free Press

Rosenstiel, L.v. (1992) Grundlagen der Organisationspsychologie, Stuttgart: Schaeffer-Poeschel

Petzall, S., Selvarajah, C. and Willis, Q. (1991) Management: A Behavioural Approach, Melbourne: Longman Cheshire

Luthans, F. (1989) Organizational behaviour, New York: McGraw-Hill

Internet

http://en.wikipedia.org/wiki/Motivation_theories accessed on 25.02.2006

http://ferl.becta.org.uk/content_files/ferl/resources/organisations/rsc_scotland/j oan_walker/motivational_theories.pp#1 accessed on 04.03.2006

http://www.maaw.info/ArticleSummaries/ArtSumHerzberg68&03.htm accessed on 27.03.2006

http://www.managers-net.com/hawthorne.html accessed on 02.03.2006 http://www.netmba.com/mgmt/ob/motivation/erg/ accessed on 20.04.2006

http://www.quotationspage.com/search.php3?homesearch=motivation accessed on 15.02.2006

http://www.quotationspage.com/search.php3?Search=Motivation&startsearch =Search&Author=&C=mgm&C=motivate&C=classic&C=coles&C=poor&C=lind sly accessed on 24.04.2006

http://www.tutor2u.net/business/gcse/people_motivation_theories.htm accessed on 25.03.2006

http://www.tutor2u.net/business/images/herzberg_factors.gif accessed on 20.03.2006

http://www.tutor2u.net/business/people/motivation_theory_herzberg.asp accessed on 25.03.2006

http://www.valuebasedmanagement.net/methods_alderfer_erg_theory.html accessed on 10.04.2006

http://www.yourquotations.net/author/Rick%20Pitino.html accessed on 25.02.2006

Journals

Wooldridge, E. (1995) "Time to stand Maslow's hierachy on its head?", People Management, Vol.1, Issue 25, p. 17

Maslow, A. (1943) "A Theory of Human Motivation", Psychological Review, 50, p. 370-396

Whittington, J.L. and Evans, B. (2005) "General Issues in Management", Problems & Perspectives in Management, Issue 2, p. 114-122

Buchanan, L. (2004) "The Things They Do for Love", Harvard Business Review, Vol. 82, Issue 12, p. 19-20

Herzberg, F. (2003) "One More Time: How Do You Motivate Employees?",
Harvard Business Review, Vol. 81, Issue 1, p. 86-96

Lightning Source UK Ltd.
Milton Keynes UK
UKOW042115140513

210672UK00001B/178/P